To my cousins Anna and Gustav

Before entering the adult world

Many adults that I have met often express the desire to work less. They want to have more vacation, downshift and maybe only work on a part-time basis, have more leisure time and the possibility to retire as early as possible. I don't know if any of them succeed in realizing that dream, or if it's only empty talk, perhaps even some form of whining. But I do know that if they were familiar with what I'm about to describe in this little writing, they would have all the necessary information to make this dream a reality. For nowadays an elegant solution exists for those who wish to cut down on work, a solution that is available to average people. I call it to "Surf the Wave."

Surf the Wave is to live on the returns from saved money. You can continue to work as before when surfing this financial wave, but the point is that you're not financially impelled to do so. This approach to living is not reserved for people who have inherited large sums of money or made windfall profits from selling off successful companies, which I assumed was the case until my eyes were opened just a few years ago. Quite the contrary, any average person can surf this wave. And the method is very simple, at least in theory.

During an initial working phase you work hard and save harder. The money you save is invested, for example in stocks through index funds. You don't need to know anything about the stock market to do this, it's very simple. This invested money is your wave. You will get return on your investments, in other words you will get paid for having saved the money. The more money you save and the lower your living costs, the sooner the payments from the wave, that is the returns from the investments, will cover your expenses. It's possible to achieve this in only 10 years. The money now works for you; you no longer need to work for money. You have gone from middle-class to kick-ass. You have a whole wave of "F-You Money", as it's called, at your disposal – this can be used to give middle fingers to employers, would there be need for it. You have created your own retirement fund and can do whatever you want for the rest of your life.

Surprisingly few people are aware that this wave is available for surf, that also a middle-class person with low income can become financially independent in a fraction of the normal working life. In my surrounding, I can only name a couple of friends who are familiar with this.

I remember for example getting into a conversation last autumn in Biarritz, France about stocks and savings with Fredrik, who was my brother's friend and someone I got to know better thanks to this trip. We were sitting on one of the big balconies with our legs hanging over the edge, with a magnificent view of the horizon of the Atlantic in front of us, and the Pyrenees in Spain to the left, as we sipped our afternoon coffee. Although Fredrik mentioned that he also speculated in commodity futures and other risky instruments that I stayed away from, I think we both had that feeling of human warmth that comes from being engaged in a conversation where you share a deep interest with a potential future friend. It was as if we were disclosing a secret we had both discovered but that few others were aware of, namely the power that comes from money put to work in investments. He confided in me that his objective was to one day have $100,000 saved up in investments. Perhaps the returns from those $100,000 could pay a vacation or two per year for him, every year – forever, he fantasized with a dreamlike look on his face.

For other middle-class Stockholmers, who struggle to have even $100 left at the end of the month, and for whom a saving of two monthly incomes is the greatest sum they could ever imagine to possibly save up for security, $100,000 would surely appear to be an overwhelming fortune. But as I heard Fredrik mention this sum I thought to myself: Why so shy ambitions? You should have one million dollars, not only $100,000. The returns from one million dollars would cover your expenses with a good margin, for the rest of your life, like an eternal retirement fund. At the time of this conversation I had already saved up $440,000, although Fredrik probably had made more money than me through his working career, and based on this amount of money I had decided to "retire" by cancelling all my consultancy jobs and instead planned to see what life had to offer for a while, making a living on frugality and the returns from my wave of $440,000.

It surprised me that a smart guy like Fredrik had discovered the magic of investing but did not envision the full potential associated with his discovery. He had understood what kind of returns to expect from investing, and had even formulated the objective that some living expenses, in this case travels, would be covered with the returns from the invested capital. That is, these costs would be surfed with the wave. He had not, however, thought one step further and realized that with only a little additional effort ALL his living expenses could be surfed with the wave. But as we shall see, it took myself quite some time to succeed with this obvious conclusion too, and it's difficult for me today to understand why I didn't attain this clear yet revolutionary insight earlier. Anyway, I didn't mention this idea and possible objective to him while on the balcony in Biarritz. I notice that I'm sometimes shy to do so, which I believe originates from a fear to hurt the individual in question. For if you have reached a certain age and accommodated with expensive habits it might be too late to start building yourself a wave. You're no longer in the right position in life, you don't have the required energy anymore. And in that case perhaps it's better to never hear about this fantastic alternative to Surf the Wave, than to be exposed to the bitterness of knowing that you had the chance but missed it.

So, Anna and Gustav, with your approaching entrance into the adult world and to the labor market in mind I now put together this little enlightenment-writing about Surf the Wave, to avoid that also you will walk about blindly like most people in my and earlier generations seem to do, and as I did myself until recently. All choices in life are still available to you, and you should of course choose whatever you want - but I want you to at least have heard about the choice to Surf the Wave.

Why Surf the Wave?

Surf the Wave means that you have created your own money-machine, and therefore don't have to work for money anymore yourself. And not only for a limited period, which is the case when you've saved up money for a longer trip or similar projects, where after the savings are gone and you're back where you started. This money-wave, instead, will cover the rest of your life.

When I was about to produce this writing I thought it would be good with some real-world examples of individuals unfamiliar with the concept of Surf the Wave but who would have been a lot better off had they known about it. I started to think about friends and contacts to find an example, and soon realized when I did this exercise that, except for one or two friends who were already informed, all of my friends and contacts would have had a great advantage in life had they known about Surf the Wave! Because it would be too extensive a chapter to present all these people here, I have chosen a few examples representing different life situations. Perhaps the advantages of Surf the Wave are completely obvious and that I now kick in open doors. Anyway, here follow some examples.

Anders is a guy from my high school class. He rents an apartment in a small city in southern Sweden together with his girlfriend, but their dream is to own a home outside of the city. A house in that area costs about $350,000, and on top of that some $700/month in average running costs. But since they both are self-employed the bank won't grant them a loan, and thus they're stuck in that shitty apartment downtown. How come they don't have their own money to overcome this financial problem? They are my age, very talented, highly educated and both are athletic and in excellent health. How is it possible that two individuals with these outstanding attributes are still broke when approaching the age of 40 years? What have they done during their lives, since finishing high school? Well, they've done what I also was doing previously. They have lived without a plan and quickly spent the money that they had temporarily accumulated. They haven't had a compass direction in life, they haven't known that there is a wave to surf. If they had known, their situation would be entirely different today. I for sure have been no star when it comes to building a wave, partly because I started way too late and partly because my salary was very low during my four initial years of work. However, if they had only performed at my low level they would have the possibility to buy that house cash today and still have enough left over of the wave to cover the monthly running costs plus food in eternity. They wouldn't be living in luxury, but it would have worked, and any additional income from random jobs would be money directly into their pockets to spend in any way they see fit. But it's probably too late for them now. They plan to have children, and with that comes additional costs and a responsibility requiring a lot of time and energy. The period in their lives of dedicating full strength to work and save and build a wave to live off is over. That train has already left. Sadly, they probably had no idea that this train was there for them to take.

Anders has a sister, Sofia, who also can serve as a good example of someone who would clearly have a better life had she had a wave to surf. Sofia detests the Swedish winter, which I guess all of us do, but she does so with special intensity and has therefore spent the past years escaping to India during the winter months. This has become a part of her lifestyle: she comes home to Sweden in the spring, works and saves up money, and then leaves for India in the autumn. I met her when I was in my hometown last summer and learned that she probably wouldn't be able to save up enough money this year, but plans to leave anyway and somehow solve the financial issue while in India. "I'd rather struggle in the woods than kit up in camp," as a friend used to say in the military, referring to the fact that he didn't care to spend energy on detailed preparations before the exercise but rather took the hit out in the wilderness. (The expression makes a beautiful alliteration with Swedish slang that I can't translate). I commented that she was brave to launch without financial security, to which she replied: In my view it's you guys who are brave to face the whole winter in Sweden. That was a quick counter comment, that I didn't agree with though. Later I also reflected on how life would be for her in the future. She was now a bit over 30 years old, still with enough energy and strength to take on new jobs every summer in Sweden. But how will it be when she gets older? How will it be when she is too weak or fragile to work at all and has to prepare for retirement? Low-paying jobs during the summers don't exactly build up a pension, she would be a case for the guaranteed pension (the minimum pension paid by the government, which is similar to Social Security), which today is about $1000/month. But then it struck me that this probably would be a huge amount of money for her, who had adapted to get by with very little to make it through each year with only the income from a couple of months' work, and I stopped worrying. Anyway: it of course sucks to work those shitty jobs during the summer in Sweden, and she has hinted that to be able to travel all the time would be ideal. With a wave to surf she could be doing just that. And given that she can get by with so little money it wouldn't have to be a big wave. Working full-time, she could probably have built it up in less than 5 years. But she didn't build up any wave. Instead, she started off wasting several years at the university and racked up student loans, and after that she has spent all the money she has earned in Sweden during the summers on her winter excursions. Thus every summer, year after year, she has to pull the horse plow of low-skilled junk jobs – the kind of jobs she disliked to the extent that this summer she had experienced physical symptoms in form of back pain and had to quit.

Johan is a guy from Gothenburg that I used to work for during my consultancy period, with whom I became good friends and still hang out with regularly. Sailing is Johan and his wife's main interest. One evening during a dinner with good food and also some wine at their place they told me about their fantasies of embarking on a worldwide sailing adventure. That idea also excited my fantasy, and it so happened that Johan and I often returned to this subject of sailing whenever we met. After a while I understood that sailing all the time, as a lifestyle, was the real dream. It was possible to get a boat for this kind of sailing for about $50,000, and according to Johan you have to count with additional monthly expenses of about $1000 for food, port fees and boat maintenance. They could imagine handling this with saved money for a 2-year around-the-world sailing trip. However, for the full sailor lifestyle they would have to wait until retirement at age 65 years. I reflected: if Johan and his wife had known how money could work for them and built up a wave together - they were a bit older than me and had high-paying jobs so it wouldn't have been impossible at all - they could realize this dream. They could buy one of those sailing boats, not a too expensive one but still one that would work for a two-person sailing adventure on the open seas, and they would have more than enough money left invested in the wave giving them returns to cover the estimated monthly expenses with a good margin. They could sail the world for the rest of their lives without concerns about the money ever running out. But since I never heard Johan mention this as an alternative to financing sailing adventures, I assume that they had no clue about it. They did start a joint savings account, though, for a potential future long-term cruise, but soon after got married and threw their wedding party abroad, which totally ruined them. So I guess the sailing adventure is as far away as ever. It's the same pattern all the time: people save up money, but then they kill the hen that could produce eggs for them, instead of feeding it and live off the eggs. They eat up their savings that could produce returns. And their dreams remain unrealized.

Olofsson is of one of my best military service friends, who recently quit his job at a bigger web bureau to start his own business. During a recent lunch we expanded our views and discussed the fact that he has let go of the safety net of being an employee, and I was curious about his intentions regarding work and what he wanted to do with his life. Being both a skilled and passionate programmer, he told me that his dream was to develop a successful app to provide him with a passive income so that he wouldn't have to work anymore but instead would have the freedom to do whatever he likes. In other words, what he wants is to surf the wave. Maybe he will succeed in creating such an app, but maybe not; it would be great if he did, but the chances are small. To work hard and save even harder during a given period, and thereby accumulate a large sum of money, on the other hand, is a very certain path to financial wave-surf. But I don't tell him about this wave approach, even though I'm his good friend since the military service almost 20 years ago. Because it's probably too late for him to build this wave. With a second child recently born the period in his life of dedicating full power to work and save and build a wave to live off is most likely over. I think the information about financial wave-surf would only make Olofsson and others like him bitter in that they missed out on this fantastic chance without even knowing it, and I therefore avoid to inform them of this alternative in life.

Pierre, a guy I got to know in the student corridor in Stockholm, and whom I still have contact with now and then, has also expressed a preference for working less and creating more leisure time. At the same time, he doesn't want to cut down on his spending. He wants a top modern car, the latest smartphone, the slickest Mac computer, the fastest road racer bike, the biggest TV and vacations to warm, sunny places in the winter. He knows precisely where his money is going, so I wonder how serious he is about this wish for an increase in leisure time. In any case, it doesn't seem to be something he gives priority to, although he of course would find it sweet if he could keep his current lifestyle without having to work. But what I wanted to point out when it comes to Pierre was a good example of the choice between having the cake and eating it; making a choice between saving some money to enjoy leisure time later vs. spending all the money directly, namely when Pierre as a student bought a car (!). My financial life during my student years was organized as such that I worked on weekends and lived very minimalistically during the winter, so that when summer came I had enough money to be free from June-August, which is the short period of summer in Sweden when I definitely didn't want to be locked up indoors. "Man, I wish I had your life!" Pierre commented several times with a mix of admiration and envy, referring to my completely free summers. So, one spring he bought that car for $2000, which happened to coincide with the sum I had saved up to make it through the summer without working. To me, the choice between having the cake and eating it couldn't be clearer, and I remember pointing this out to Pierre when he demonstrated his car for me outside the student corridor: you do understand that you've just swopped your whole summer freedom for this car? (And even more, because a car has many hidden costs as well, but at the time I wasn't aware of that.) He mumbled something briefly half in shame, and then continued to show the car's features and finesses.

Finally, I want to take as a general example all the young people who have recently entered the labor market, people from my age group and younger. The new Swedish pension system has shown to result in pretty thin retirement pensions, especially for those who only worked part-time jobs or didn't have an occupational pension in their employment contracts. Also, the politicians in Europe are currently discussing increasing the retirement age given that the baby boomers will retire and a small working portion of the population will be forced to support this larger portion of retirees. I think many in my generation and the younger generation who have just started a working career have feelings of hopelessness when it comes to retirement, related both to the prospect that life as a retiree probably will be poor and to the uncertainty as to when working life will come to an end – now there are discussions about increasing the retirement age from 65 to 67 years, but who knows how much more it has to be increased for the system to function 30 years from now, when it is time for my generation to retire? Put Surf the Wave in contrast to this retirement anxiety: If you can learn to live a smart and low-cost lifestyle and put away at least half of your income from paid work, which is totally possible in rich countries today even with the worst paying jobs, your expected working life is not 40 years or 50 years or however long you can fear it to be, but only 10 years. Just consider that for a moment. After 10 years of work-hard-save-harder you can retire, with your home-made pension fund, and do whatever you want for the rest of your life.

*

I'm convinced that a lot of people in my surroundings would have better lives had they surfed the wave. But they have no clue that this alternative approach exists, and now it's too late for them. They have bought expensive houses and cars, they have gotten married and have kids, they have adapted to certain habits and a certain level of comfort. They are a bit over 30 years old and no longer have the energy of youth and the abundance of time to build up a surfing wave. Had they received information about Surf the Wave in their 20s, maybe their lives would have been completely different today. That's why I want to share with you my thoughts in this little writing, for you to at least have heard of this before it's too late also for you, if it turns out that you would be interested in Surf the Wave.

Anna and Gustav, my dear cousins, what do you want to do with your lives? What do you want to spend your time doing in the future? What do you want to work with? What objectives will you have in life? Anna, you have mentioned becoming an author. Most people who try that are not able to support themselves and are forced to work low-paying side jobs to make ends meet, which might be romantic in youth but as you get older, and in addition have kids, it's nothing but miserable. I propose: get a job, any job will do, work hard and save harder for 10 years, then you will be financially independent and can pursue your dreams as an author for the rest of your life, whether you get paid for it or not! Go to university if you like, but make sure that the years you lose there pay off later in the form of better-paying jobs, as an investment. If you're attracted to a university environment for the intellectual development it offers, you can nowadays find everything for free online or in the library. And don't worry, you will have time and energy to write quite a bit also while working, during that initial intensive period. Gustav, you enjoy computers, gaming and programming. You have mentioned that you'd like to become a YouTuber like PewDiePie, which perhaps was a youthful wish that you have already left behind. But I can imagine that you would prefer something like Olofsson in the previous example, that is some passive income from a successful effort and based on that live the sweet life. I think that's what we all want in our hearts. Your parents stress somewhat stubbornly and also worryingly that a YouTuber is not a smart career choice given that very few make it, and I fully agree. The same applies to those apps Olofsson dreams to create. You only see the few who succeed, you don't see the thousands of losers who try but fail, and the risk is high that you will just become one of those losers if you take that path. Again, my advice is: get a job, any job, work hard and save harder for 10 years, then you're done. That's a much more certain path to the sweet life.

How do you achieve
Surf the Wave?

But is it really true that one can retire after as little as 10 years of being in the workforce? Normal working life is 40 years or more, so it does seem pretty extreme to drop out already after only 10 years. Sure, you hear about people who live off capital, but aren't those people celebrities who have made billions of dollars? Or lucky ones who have inherited a fortune? Or entrepreneurs who in a windfall gain made a huge sum of money when selling their successful businesses? Or random dare-devils who jeopardized the family's savings on some high-risk stock and happened to win? For average people, people like you and me, ordinary middle-class people with typical jobs – is it really possible also for us to live this free man's life after only 10 years of work?

The answer is yes. But it requires an initial period, 10 years can suffice, of hard work and even harder saving to build up a wave for surf, and that one's lifestyle continues to be within the limits of this wave. You have to make sure that your living expenses are covered by the returns from your money, in order not to start munching on the capital itself. Only eat the eggs from the hen; do not kill the hen to have an additional feast, because then there will be no more eggs. Then you'll have to go back to the slavery that dependence on paid employment really is.

Saving in stocks has historically given an average annual return of about 7%, after accounting for inflation. Some years of course a lot more, and some a lot less, but over time an average of about 7%. With that level of return you can surf the wave already after 11 years of work, if you're able to save half of your income. That is: if you manage to have half of your salary left at the end of each month, and put this money in stocks with a 7% annual growth, you can quit your job after 11 years. The 7% of the growth of your money is reinvested during these 11 years in parallel with new money coming in from your salary, but after 11 years you can terminate your paid work and start withdrawing the 7% return to cover all your yearly living expenses the rest of your life. If you're annual income is $40,000 after tax, and you're able to live off half of that ($20,000) while investing the other half in stocks, you have a wave of a bit more than $315,000 after 11 years (based on 7% annual return, reinvested). 7% of $315,000 is $22,050, which is more than you need for living ($20,000). If you keep the same lifestyle that previously cost you half of your income ($20,000), you can now stop working in that your wave gives you more than this in return

($22,050). And note that this is not for a limited period. If you don't withdraw more from the wave than its growth (7%), the size of the wave is maintained and it will provide you with the $22,050 every year, for the rest of your life.

In this way, with a bit of planning and discipline, your "prison sentence" in the labor market can be shortened substantially. And it doesn't take a fancy job with a fat salary to achieve this goal. Initiation of surf is not determined by the size of your salary, but by the proportion of the salary that you can save. If you make $80,000 per year instead of $40,000 as in the previous example, and save half of this income to invest in stocks, your estimated working life is still 11 years. After 11 years you will have a wave of about $630,000, which at a 7% return gives you $44,100 per year. This amount is greater than what you spent on living while working, so if you maintain that cost level you can now surf the wave.

The reason why it takes the same time to reach surf even when the income is twice as high is that the living expenses in that example were twice as high as well, which required a twofold increase in the wave. In fact, how many years you have to spend on the labor market before you can start surfing boils down to one single variable, namely the proportion of your salary that you can save. If you can save 60% instead of 50%, as in the previous examples, you can decrease your working life from 11 to 8 years, irrespective of income level. If you make $80,000 per year as in the second example, but have living expenses of $20,000 as in the first example, that is you save 75% of your income, your estimated working life is only 5 years.

*

These calculations based on a 7% steady annual growth and withdrawal at surf should be viewed as simplifications to introduce the general idea. In reality, achieving surf is a bit more complex and less predictable.

One simplification is that the 7% withdrawal from the stocks is presumed to be tax-free, whereas in real life income from capital is often taxed at 30%. But there are legal ways to avoid large parts of this tax. In Sweden, for example, there are tax-advantaged accounts where you pay 30% tax on a small assumed profit (currently 1.25%), regardless of your real profits. In addition, instead of investing directly in an index fund you can buy a future's contract with leverage based on the index. With this scheme, you only need to have 15% of your money in the tax-advantaged account, which means that only 15% of your money will be subjected to that assumed profit and taxed while the other portion (85%) avoids this taxation and can even earn (taxed) interest on a savings account with deposit insurance guaranteed by the government (such as FDIC insurance). The profits from your investment, however, are unchanged as though 100% would be working in the tax-advantaged account. There are some transaction costs related to this method, but the resulting effective tax becomes very low. This strategy is just one method of return optimization that I have happened to come across, there are probably several other and better ways. I refer to the Stock Series on JL Collins' blog for similar arrangements in the USA.

Another simplification is the assumed steady growth of the stock market, while in real life it often shows frightening volatility. Given the risk of temporary poor stock market performance, and even stock market crashes, you might be forced to eat parts of the hen (your main capital) during bad years. Strategies can be used to limit this danger, however. The American surfer JL Collins suggests that once you have your wave built, you could have 25% of your capital in bonds (lone-based investments that grow a lot slower but are more stable). During bad stock market periods, which normally don't last longer than 3 years, you surf on this reserve instead. When the stock market recovers you rebalance to 75% stocks/25% bonds again.

Another approach is to plan for a lower withdrawal rate from your stocks. In the surfer community 4% is often proposed as a conservative estimate of how much you continuously can drain your wave and at the same time avoid running dry, instead of the 7% in my examples. This number originates from simulations of scenarios with start of surf at different time points in history, which include situations where one is assumed to quit work and instead raise on the board to surf off the stock investments just before a stock market crash. The results showed that if you don't drain your wave with more than 4% during good years, and don't eat more than 4% of the hen during bad years, chances are very high that the wave will suffice through life (and in many cases also grow substantially in size). With this more careful withdrawal rate, the length of your working life becomes 15 years if you save half of your income, 12 years if you save 60% and 7 years if you save 75%.

A third approach, which can be combined with the other two, is to be a flexible surfer. If the stock market crashes, avoid traveling around the world precisely that year, or even take up a bit of paid work, if frugality alone is not enough.

The calculations used in my examples with a steady annual growth of the stock market and no tax on the returns may appear to be overly optimistic. But objections from these grounds only consider the work-life length, not the principle of surf itself; they are about giving or taking a couple of years in your expected time to surf. I want to claim that by using the stock market as a power engine you can exit the work market well before your 40th birthday, even with substantial safety margins around the wave, if you can only save at least half of your income. Many people have actually achieved this, although they are not commonly known.

*

When it comes to Surf the Wave, it's better to focus on becoming a lightweight surfer with low costs because such a surfer does not require a big wave. To build up a big wave that can handle high living costs requires a high income, which can be difficult to achieve. You may have to make a career, and perhaps in a specific field, whereas cutting down on costs is a simple task anybody can undertake with success. High living costs are like weights attached to your legs while surfing: you end up deeper in the water, it's harder to accelerate when you paddle, and the waves are not powerful enough to move you forward. The waves roll by while you paddle to exhaustion. For a lightweight surfer, on the other hand, few paddle strokes are needed to gain speed, and then the rolling power of the waves suffices to carry the surfer forward.

You should therefore focus on an efficient and frugal low-cost lifestyle rather than chasing big money in the hope of maintaining expensive habits. In this context, it's better to focus on having a defensive strategy to an offensive one. It doesn't matter how many goals you score (how high income you have) if you have huge holes in your defense line and let just as many goals be scored against you (high living costs).

I had the same experience when I tried to learn how to swim front crawl a couple of years ago, with pretty poor results. It wasn't so much the power to move forward that I lacked, I believe, but rather the flexibility in the shoulders to achieve a better floating angle and to position the whole body along the surface of the water and thereby limit drag. With my stiff shoulders preventing a correct body position, I swam like a plow through the water, which required extreme muscular force to move forward. For every new arm stroke I had lost speed and had to re-accelerate the forward motion of my body. This is how financial life is for most people. They struggle hard but don't get ahead; all their power is consumed but they stand still. They would glide through life better, had they removed some drag (costs). And if the power of a light wave would be added, they soon wouldn't need to swim at all to move forward.

It should also be stressed that no special knowledge about stocks or the stock market is needed to build up a wave, which many people seem to believe when they hear about this. When they learn that people with totally normal jobs have built up several hundreds of thousands of dollars in savings, they think that this has only been possible because of some magic stock market tricks, that they themselves un-fortunately do not know about. However, it doesn't require any specific knowledge about stocks or the stock market to build up a wave; you don't need to be educated in finance or study the quarterly reports of corporations or follow the international financial news. You just need to know one thing about the stock market: that you know nothing. Like Socrates was pointed out by the oracle to be the wisest of all persons because he acknowledged that he knew nothing, this insight is enough: I don't know which stocks will go up or down in the future, and neither do you. Therefore you spread out your savings over the whole world and all kinds of businesses using low-cost index funds.

Surf the Wave is not painful to achieve

Are you then supposed to torture yourself working and saving hard during the best years of life, while others travel and party and enjoy life? Are you supposed to submit to self-mortification as Martin Luther did during his initial period as a monk in which he repeated prayers throughout the night while kneeling on a hard, stone floor in the cellar of a monastery? And then continue this self-denial for the rest of your life by arranging your lifestyle according to the poor returns of a surfing wave, to shorten your period of paid work?

That is perhaps how wave-building and subsequent surfing may appear to a beginner, and it therefore seems impossible to on the one hand "enjoy life" and on the other to save money to build up a wave. However, your life doesn't have to differ that much from the lives of others to build up a wave in a short time; perhaps an external observer wouldn't even be able to tell from a glance who is building a wave and who is living from paycheck to paycheck, steadily running the bank account to the bottom every month. All you need to do is to inject a dose of reason to your activities, for them to be organized and performed cost-effectively. You can enjoy life just as others, but thanks to that you reflect a bit about how things can be done in the best way, and in this case the best way means the way with the lowest costs, you end up with a large portion of your income left each month, and the wave can be built.

Moreover, it may provide pleasure to strive and hustle. I personally often think to notice how feelings of happiness and satisfaction arise from the sharp contrast in the transition from hardship to comfort. Hike in the mountains and then notice how fantastic a typical shower and sauna is, rather than going to a luxury spa to experience this pleasure. Perform a hard physical workout and enjoy simple food, instead of chilling out the whole day and then go to a fancy restaurant to achieve a pleasurable food experience. In fact, it's not far-fetched to suggest that the simple and frugal life with muscles instead of motors for private matters and time for yourself and friends instead of shopping represents the good life, and if you just figure out the techniques of this lifestyle the wave will build up by itself, as a positive side-effect, whether you want it or not, given that this life is also a low-cost life.

Cost-effectiveness: streamline your life
To strive for cost-effectiveness is the key to building a wave and at the same time enjoy life as everybody else. With cost-effectiveness I mean that for all situations you reflect over how

the activity can be financially optimized, as well as realize that some activities come with such high costs that they are not worth pursuing.

To go to the cinema, for example, is a pleasant activity, and the accompanying cost of $8 doesn't make a big hole in the wallet. Maybe $10 or $12 would be acceptable too, if the movie is good. But $20 starts to become expensive, and nobody would pay $100. In that case it's not worth the money anymore; it's no longer cost-effective. You'd rather spend the money on something else or save it.

This way of thinking is simply common sense. Not to strive for cost-effectiveness in the field of private finances is in fact irrational. It's like dumping money into the sea, which doesn't feel good for those who otherwise believe in reason to be the best guide in life. In other words: not to pursue cost-effectiveness is to be foolish, which doesn't feel good for those who in other areas try to avoid being foolish.

With cost-effectiveness as a guiding principle you remove all the unnecessary, and keep only the necessary. You filter away the noise, and keep the signal. Just like you clean out your closet and get rid of everything you don't use anyway; like losing weight and liberating yourself from superfluous fat, which is a burden in itself and causes illnesses; like writing short and elegant programming code that is efficient and easy to understand, without waffling rubbish.

To strive for cost-effectiveness is very simple. You only need to do the following:

1. Identify the purpose of the activity. What constitutes the core?

2. Figure out how this purpose can be achieved most efficiently, that is with as low costs as possible.

For example, when I'm about to meet my friend Per, a very inspiring wave builder, the purpose is to engage in good conversation. This is usually combined with dinner at his or my place because it's a pleasure to talk over dinner, and we have to eat anyway. It could be a good idea to have dinner at a restaurant instead, if you value the service, environment and food experience a restaurant offers. In that case this is also a purpose, and the question is how you fulfill this activity at the lowest possible cost. But for us that kind of experience has no special value, and therefore dinner at home is good enough. In addition, the food we prepare is cheap, tasty and nutritious. To prepare something expensive, or to have dinner at an expensive restaurant, wouldn't contribute with any value to our experience. It would only be an additional cost, without an additional positive effect, in short: it would be less cost-effective. The money we both avoid losing on non-cost-effective dinners are pumped straight into our waves, yet we are just as satisfied as those who choose to burn their money at restaurants.

My Europe roundtrip by car the summer I was 23 years old when I just came out of the military in June with $6000 cash in my pocket can serve as another example to shed light on the concept of cost-effectiveness. I bought an Audi 100 with a couple of friends and drove south through Germany and along the coast of France, then over to Spain and further to Italy, down to Sardinia where we stayed at a friend's place for 10 days to eat and recover, and so up to the Italian Alps, then straight-up through Europe and east to the Baltics. I wasn't back in Stockholm until mid August, with only about $100 left of the initial $6000.

    That was a great summer adventure with my friends, no doubt. But could it have been performed more wisely? What was the purpose of the trip? Was the purpose to have an exciting joint experience with a car, where we slept in bushes and other places we hid at, and enjoy the unpredictable life of adventurers? If so, maybe it wouldn't have been necessary to drive all the way down to southern Europe, it could have sufficed to stay in the northern countries and have the same experience at a lower cost. Was the purpose to visit large parts of Europe? If so, maybe interrail would have been a smarter alternative. Perhaps the purpose was something else, or a mix of the two; in any case I was at the time probably unaware of any of these purposes, I guess it simply seemed "fun" without any further reflections. I don't know. But I do know that if I would have limited myself to burn only half of the money that summer, and invested the other half, that is $3000, it could have been worth more than $8000 today (based on a 7% annual return that is reinvested, not inflated), which is a substantial sum of money to be included in the wave.

This trip was just one in a long list of stupid trips I made, where without insight in cost-effectiveness or the power of money I repeatedly spent all my savings. And I believe I'm not alone in this respect. I suspect that traveling for many is an activity that consumes a lot of confused money and opportunities. Although I used to do the same, I often get shocked when I hear how much money people spend on trips - people who otherwise are broke or even have a negative net worth when considering their debt.

Finally, regarding the concept of cost-effectiveness I'd like to mention the category where you find the most astonishing examples of non-cost-effective activities, namely weddings. And I'm not talking about the absurd arrangements of rich Hollywood stars, because those people are often absurd in all other aspects as well. I'm talking about the typical weddings of the middle-class. A wedding can be a fantastic party, for sure, nothing less would be expected when you gather friends and family for a happy celebration with food and drinks and speeches and music under the same roof on a summer night. It's a great party, and the memories provide joy for years to come. But the bill for this party often ends up in the area of $20-30,000, possibly even twice that sum if the costs related to gifts as well as travel and housing for the guests are considered. That would be the same as paying $2000 to go to the cinema – fun, sure, but is it reasonable to spend that amount of money in this way? Maybe it would be possible to organize just as good a party with the same guests and have just as much fun for only a fraction of the cost? But, as David Henry Thoreau observed in the USA in the 19th century as well: the middle-class sees what the rich do, and wants to do the same. That explains the elegant clothing, the floral arrangements, the crystal glasses and the silver cutlery; that explains the paid photographer, the paid serving staff, the paid musicians; that explains the gifts; that explains all this royal non-cost-effective expensive nonsense that doesn't add any value. The problem is people from the middle-class can't afford this, and as a consequence have to continue to sell their bodies and souls to paid work until old age, while their lips mumble that most of all they would like to cut down on work and have more time for leisure.

*

In summary: To achieve Surf the Wave, apply a mindset of cost-effectiveness to everything you do. Lead a simple, minimalistic and frugal life. You'll notice that you'll be happier than most people while money from your salary piles up in your bank account. Put this money to work in the stock market. Somewhere between 30 and 40 years of age you can retire from paid work and start to think about what you really want to do with your life.

My own story

I myself didn't discover the idea of Surf the Wave until I was 32 years old, which was about 10 years too late. At this age most surfers already start to raise on their surfboards and leave the workforce. Luckily, though, I knew since childhood how to cut costs and draw my bow hard towards future objectives, and in early adulthood I practiced a low-cost lifestyle that I later held on to. In this way my wave started to build up unintentionally already 4 years earlier, at the age of 28 years, and once I had found the path of Surf the Wave it was easy for me to adapt to its philosophy.

As a 12-year-old, I recall being seized by a strong desire to buy a tent, and not just any tent, but a tunnel tent of the best model – one of those that my uncle had used when he kayaked from Stockholm down to us in the southern end of Sweden (>500 km in the Baltic Sea), an adventure and achievement I greatly admired. The tent cost $400, which at the time was a huge sum of money for a 12-year-old, and the situation was further complicated because few jobs were available for kids of my age. You heard about kids in the neighborhood who could get a dollar or two for mowing the lawn or other garden work, but this happened to be my dad's favorite work, so that was not a possibility of income for me. I think I started to deliver journals at this point, making about $20-30 per month which together with my weekly allowance constituted my revenue. But to save up those $400 over the winter for the next summer, when I wanted the tent, I most of all had to cut expenses. I don't think I bought anything at all during that whole autumn and winter and spring, but instead saved every single penny and followed with a chart on the fridge how the accumulated savings slowly but surely approached the cost of the tent. When summer came I had the money, and bought the tent.

Now, afterward, I think of this challenge of buying the tent as the best thing my parents could have ever given me. It would have been no problem for them to just buy me that tent, but by forcing me to save up money for it myself I gained grit and mental muscles, that have proven to be very useful later in life. The tent is still in good condition, by the way, today 25 years later, and delivered cozy and safe nights when I hiked in Sarek (a protected wilderness area in the mountains north of the polar circle in Sweden) last September.

Another period that from many perspectives, including a wave-surfer perspective, had a positive character-shaping effect was when I performed the military service (mandatory at the time in Sweden) at the Armed Forces Parachute Ranger School. Just to be admitted to this service I needed to nurture my grit and mental muscles and draw my soul's bow hard. During the training itself these characteristics were further strengthened through the several 24-hour-long physical tests that were formal requirements for approval, and which pushed our ideas of what we were capable of way beyond our prior limits, and through the long and tough exercises when we were dropped by parachute deep into the forests of the wilderness north of the polar circle with only what we had in our backpacks to survive on for several weeks. I can't say nothing else than that I after completing the military service was well equipped to toughen up financially and swiftly build up a wave to surf on for the rest of my life. But I had no clue that this alternative lifestyle even existed.

When I came out from the military service, 21 years old, my plan for life was instead to alter intensive but short periods of work with longer periods of travel. I imagined that with the grit and self-discipline I had refined at the Parachute Ranger School, working hard for a couple of months in exchange for money to save up for maybe over a year of traveling would be no match. However, it turned out that not only were the jobs that I ended up doing (substitute teacher in primary school and employee at a petrol station) monotonous and soul-sucking in a way I hadn't expected, but also the money I was able to put away during a semester of disciplined work and hard saving was burnt during an even shorter period in Brazil. I left at the beginning of January; already 3 months later I was back again with most of my money spent. And I surely wasn't motivated to take on the horse plow of low-skilled jobs once again.

I went for the military again, and then embarked on university studies with some vague idea that there would at least be less painful jobs at the end of it, and maybe even more pay per hour. With no defined long-term objectives for my life, and no clear picture of any meaning either, I allocated all my resources to the fashion of the time - travels and excitements. I made sure to live simply and minimalistically as a student and worked on the weekends (but had work-free summers), in order to later finance some longer travel during winter, most often to Brazil, where my savings went up in smoke like a New Year's Eve firework.

I thought I was smart to live like this, to save hard and then travel. Today, I can objectively comment that I was not. Or, to be fair: I was perhaps smarter than many others, who mindlessly spent their money on coffee downtown, eating at restaurants, having drinks at bars, purchasing expensive clothes and other stupidities, while at the same time frustrated that they never had money to travel and seek excitement, which I believe at the time was, and probably still is, a general idea of how to best spend your time on earth, how to max out your life. But I could have been much smarter, had I only known about financial wave-surf.

This went on until I was 28 years old. Until then I was like most people, that is a short-sighted and unenlightened excitement-seeker. I was therefore also broke, like most people. The only positive consequence this stupid activity of altering periods of hard saving with periods of indulgence on travels had was that during the saving periods back home in Sweden I subjected myself to the simplicity and toughness of an efficient way of life – something I eventually became pretty good at and also learned to enjoy. Despite wasting all my savings like Monopoly money during my travels, the longer periods between these trips resulted in the consolidation of a striving and hard-working lifestyle. This frugal lifestyle, in which I optimized every activity with maximum efficiency so that I could enjoy life just as much as everybody else but to a fraction of the cost – this lifestyle in combination with the initiation of a normal working-life with a paycheck every month and vacations limited to 5 weeks per year, which was too short a period for me to succeed in spending all my money on travels like before and therefore prevented my foolishness – these two factors in interaction resulted in money accruing in my bank account at a rapid rate. I was 28 years old when this started, when my wave began to build. For a couple of years this went on without any specific objective but merely as an unintended consequence of the fact that I liked and kept my simple lifestyle while new money streamed into my bank account at the end of each month.

*

At the age of about 32 years I had my eureka-experience when I finally realized the enormous power of money and the fantastic prospect of financial wave-surf. I can still vividly recall this occasion.

I was standing in my campervan with my laptop on the kitchen bench, on that black part of glass that served as a cover to the stove itself. I was wearing full clothing - winter boots, the Gore-Tex trousers with long johns under, a thick sweater with a shell jacket over, and a warm hat. It was winter outside, but because there was no wind inside the campervan my fingers could swiftly move over the keyboard without getting frozen and stiff. I performed a couple of simple calculations in Excel using two variables: annual return in percentage and total capital. The result from this calculation was then divided by 12, to represent monthly income, which was easier to relate my running expenses to. By now, I had come to understand that it was possible to get several percent of continuous return from money; I had soon recognized that the large Swedish companies I owned stocks in paid me a dividend of about 4% every spring. Initially this money that suddenly appeared on my account surprised me in that I didn't know what a dividend was. I thought the only return from stocks was from selling at a higher price than they had been bought at, but I eventually learned about dividends and looked forward to the 4% monetary "gift" from my stocks every spring. That was one of the variables in my calculation. The other variable was my total capital, which had accumulated to almost $100,000 owing to a regular income from a low-paying job combined with frugality and the stock market. A 4% return per year on $100,000 was $4000; $4000 per year was $333 per month.

$333 was not a large sum of money to pay for monthly expenses. In fact, it was well below the poverty line in Sweden at the time ($1250 per month, defined as 50% of the median income). However - and this made the whole difference – I knew this was a sum that would allow me to make a living. I owned the campervan, in which

I also lived, and could park it for free; I knew since student life, when I took note of all food expenses, that I could have good food for less than $120 per month; I knew from childhood when I saved for my tent that I could refrain from other consumption for long periods; and I knew from my former parachute ranger training that in case of necessity I could always just grit my teeth and set an iron strong will, courage and endurance. The sum of $333 would cover all my monthly expenses, if I just hustled, and if I would move to a poorer country, for example to a country in Asia, I could even live a fairly luxurious life based on this sum. And these $333 would be pumped out by my capital on a regular basis, without decreasing itself, for the rest of my life, like a perpetual motion machine.

I had discovered the magic of Surf the Wave, and it got me all carried away that dark and cold night in the campervan. My experience was perhaps not as intensive as the one of the carpenter described in the book "Your Money or Your Life", who at a seminar got his eyes opened to Surf the Wave and because of this new insight got so excited that his heart rate quickened, his palms became sweaty, his energy levels soared and he started yelling "Yes! Yes! Yes!" while laughing and crying at the same time. My experience did not have as strong expressions, but I do consider the discovery I made that night, when several key pieces of the jigsaw puzzle suddenly fell into position, as one of the major milestones of my life. I became greatly aroused in the campervan that evening by this breakthrough and felt how I was filled with a warm and cozy feeling of satisfaction and hope for the future. I think it was a combination of the fantastic opportunities that opened up and that before this night I couldn't even imagine that something like this was possible for people like me from the middle-class: the ultimate freedom, the freedom to do whatever you want for the rest of your life, to not be forced to work for money anymore even for a single day, and that all this was within reach for me.

On this occasion I had missed that I would have to pay 30% capital tax on the return used in my calculation, as I had not yet learned about the tax-advantaged accounts. So the $333 that would already prove a tough challenge to subsist on was in fact an overestimation. But at long last I had discovered Surf the Wave, and I set the goal to save up $400,000. A return of 4% - which as I have previously mentioned is a reasonable estimate of what kind of return you can expect to continuously receive from stocks without risking the main capital – on a capital of $400,000 was $16,000 per year, or $1333 per month. Such a return would cover my monthly expenses with good margin. Last year, when I was 37 years old and had spent 9 years working, I was approaching the goal of accumulating $400,000 and therefore started to dismantle my paid work. But apparently I didn't do this fast enough, for I overshot the goal and ended up with $440,000 for my "retirement", which as I write this has increased to $480,000.

Expanding my view and looking upon my previous working life, I see that it was always about a flight from pain. It started with those low-skilled jobs as a substitute teacher and at the petrol station, where every minute was torture. After the university studies I was employed in a PhD program, where the daily activity of thinking, reading, calculating and writing suited me, but where I couldn't see any meaning with the projects and where I had so little respect for management, except for my closest supervisor, all the way up to the principal that eventually I came to detest everything about the place for most of the 4 years I worked there. After that, I started my own business and worked as a consultant for 5 years, which was an enormous improvement in terms of pay and perceived freedom. Yet it was nothing but a golden jail. Those were improvements within the frames of forced labor. I always worked on the agenda of somebody else; in principle, I was nothing but a prostitute, although I could choose my clients, had stimulating tasks and received decent pay.

Now, backed by my wave, I intend to approach work from the right perspective. I will ask myself: What do I want to do? What do I find important? What do I find meaningful? How do I want to spend my time? Who do I want to hang out with? What do I want to improve? What do I want to accomplish? When I have figured that out, the subsequent question will be: Can I somehow make this activity work as a business? That would of course be ideal; then I would have arranged my dream job. But if not - no problem, I have my wave to surf on anyway. I no longer need the income from a paying job. Work turns into what is called a "hobby" or "unpaid work." "Work," which is associated with compulsion given that financial necessity forces you into it, is gone. And I don't miss it at all.

What if everybody would Surf the Wave?

But – you might now wonder, or others might wonder and ask you – what would happen if everybody lived like this, if everybody would Surf the Wave? Somebody has to work, society is based on people working. Should we close down all schools, hospitals and courts? Should we dismantle the Armed Forces? And wouldn't an economic collapse be the result if people stopped consuming and instead lead such a frugal life, with a deep recession and high unemployment as a consequence? Furthermore, isn't this surf-the-wave-talk a form of hypocrisy: to advocate a simple low-cost lifestyle but at the same time live off the returns from stocks, which originate from other people who don't have this lifestyle but actually spend their money on the various products of different companies?

Some would argue that there is no point discussing this because it seems the lifestyle of Surf the Wave only suits a tiny fraction of the population. But to elevate one's actions to universal law, in other words that others can act in the same way and the action would still be desirable, has been proposed as a moral criterion for actions by such influential philosophers as Immanuel Kant and Peter Singer. The question of what would happen to society and the economy if everybody surfed the wave should therefore be taken seriously. I do not claim to be an expert in the field, but because I haven't found a thorough discussion and in-depth analysis elsewhere, I present my thoughts on this issue here.

Economic collapse

A mass transit to wave-surf would have an impact on consumption patterns, that is obvious. However, this doesn't have to imply that industries become suddenly worthless overnight or that large masses of workers suddenly stand idle with no income. What is considered necessary for the economy to produce would change, but as long as this change does not come in an instant, the economy would have sufficient time to adapt. For it's not possible to immediately start surfing the wave, it takes about a decade to get there. Piecemeal changes provide opportunities for the markets to adapt and for politicians to act against negative consequences, even if the sum of all these small changes grows big over time. I understand the concern, but I consider it unlikely that widespread wave-surf would cause an economic collapse.

Hypocrisy

I have noticed that calling Surf the Wave hypocrisy is a common and spontaneous reaction of people who first hear about this idea, and I see what they mean. If I don't spend my money on champagne, say, but instead save it to buy stocks in the champagne producing company, I can eventually surf the wave with the returns from these stocks as long as others continue drinking champagne. But if they take after me, it wouldn't work anymore because profits from the champagne company would no longer be generated. If I persuade people to live the same frugal lifestyle as I do and abstain from drinking champagne, I would be cutting the branch on which I was sitting.

Of course I can follow this reasoning, but it's based on a narrow and superficial perspective of the economy. I think that as soon as one applies deeper thinking into what wealth and money is, this objection evaporates. For consumption does not create wealth, production does. To uphold spending for its own sake is not what makes us rich, efficient production of what we consider necessary and demand is.

My perspective is this: What is produced in the economy is distributed to the workers and the owners of the capital. By working and saving hard for a period, you become one of the owners. The production in an economy of surfers might have a different constitution or even shrink, but only because of a corresponding shift in preferences and demand. What the economy produces will still be distributed to the workers and owners. If you just make sure to be one of the owners, you won't have to exchange your time in the form of work to get your share.

Can we all be frugal, and still Surf the Wave? I can't see why this would be impossible. Perhaps the increased competition for ownership could prolong the time it takes to work your way up and become a surfer, but this does not wreck the basic principle of Surf the Wave.

Work crucial for society

Who should work then, if everybody is surfing? Where should the staffs come from who, for example, work in schools and hospitals? The short answer is: from the pool of people building their wave. A longer answer could discuss increased automation with robots and artificial intelligence, as well as the fact that a society that consumes less also needs to produce less. However, a related but more serious problem I see for a society of wave surfers is the potential difficulty to appoint positions of high importance for society, such as experienced physicians, judges, engineers and military officers. To work hard for 10 years while building the wave is not enough to develop sufficient skills for these occupations at the same time as society relies on them. This potential problem is waved aside by bloggers in the field, who argue that the time after "retirement" is the period when the true work starts: that's when you dare to work with what you're passionate about, and therefore have a good chance of becoming really skilled at, to the benefit of others; that's when you dare to start up your own business and unleash your creativity for innovation, the main driver of economic development.

This hypothesis does not immediately convince me, but my own observations in the academic field, where I worked for a period, support it. You could see old professors very passionate about their work, for whom this work was the main interest in life, and who continued to contribute with their competence and experience way beyond retirement age, and who ultimately had to be forced to leave their position. With huge pensions waiting for them, it was obvious that this was not about money. Benjamin Franklin also comes to my mind, the guy who in the 18th century worked his way up from poverty to wave-surf through his enterprising work as an editor and printer, and who despite being financially independent early in life didn't succumb to idleness but, on the contrary, continued to a completely new level and served his society, country and the whole of humanity through disciplined and efficient work as a statesman, diplomat and scientist until his death. Elon Musk, known from Tesla and SpaceX, who made a fortune when he sold PayPal at a young age, is another example. I would guess he's working more now as a surfer than ever before.

It could be that bloggers such as Mr Money Mustache have a point when they claim that the better part of one's working life starts when surfing the wave. But I still consider the question of who should carry important occupations in a society of wave surfers to be the main critique of this lifestyle.

*

There is no doubt that a transition to widespread surfing, like all bigger changes, would come with some negative consequences. But these potential disadvantages have to be compared with the potential advantages.

The environment
One important advantage of widespread surfing is a lower pressure on the earth's ecosystems. How the ecosystems will handle the burden of

ever more people getting rich and starting to enjoy the resource-intensive Western lifestyle is one of the great challenges of our time. This relates not only to climate change, but also to other factors including deforestation, loss of species and eutrophication. Recent research suggests that the safety boundaries of several important factors affecting the health of ecosystems have already been transgressed due to human activity, and corresponding boundaries of other factors are on their way to be transgressed (see for example Steffen W, Richardson K, Rockstrom J, et al. Sustainability. Planetary boundaries: guiding human development on a changing planet. Science. 2015;347 (6223):1259855). This increases the risk of ecosystems to flip to new states, or even collapse, resulting in new and perhaps substantially worse conditions for human civilization.

The problem is that the underlying cause of the transgression of these boundaries is the rich Western lifestyle. Many environmental problems at a local level, such as poor air quality in cities and polluted water for drinking and cooking, are on the contrary improved when a society becomes more economically efficient and richer. Unfortunately, the larger global environmental problems are a consequence of the most advanced and productive economies, which in all other aspects provide the best conditions for humans. Thanks to economic development billions of people are now rising from poverty and enjoying the fruits of this rich life, which will push the joint effect of human activity further beyond the ecosystems' safety limits that have already been passed, and perhaps push us over some of the limits that have not yet been passed. The tough challenge for our and coming generations is therefore to organize that we on the one hand have access to the high quality of life a productive economy provides, and on the other make sure that we are well within the safety boundaries of the ecosystems in order not to risk destroying the foundation of our civilization and economy.

This will probably require contributions from all directions: from new technology, from alternative policies and from changes in lifestyle. I believe surfers would make a strong contribution to the latter. The efficient lifestyle of a surfer does not only lead to more money in the pocket, more leisure time, improved health and increased wellbeing, but also to a decreased ecological footprint. I consider this aspect a very important potential for widespread surfing.

Stability in the economy

Another positive consequence is that Surfland would enjoy a higher degree of stability in the economy. If we all live within our means and have a substantial financial buffer, society would not be impacted as much from changes in the economy. Periods of increased unemployment, for example, would not pose the same threat in a society of surfers as in our current societies. With a wave to surf, or with the beginning of a wave to temporarily live off during a hard period of unemployment, no drastic interventions from the government and no dramatic changes of the unemployed individuals' situation would be needed.

In addition, I would expect fewer financial crises as that which occurred in 2008, when the American housing bubble imploded, causing financial shock waves worldwide with huge economic problems as a consequence, which in turn stirred up discontent and anger and even led to protests and riots, as well as prepared the ground for populist right-wing movements to germinate and start growing. This whole crisis, the consequences of which we still have to deal with 10 years later, was rooted in the tendency of people who don't have money to live as if they did. Had these people been surfers, they wouldn't have bought a house they couldn't afford; had these people been surfers, they wouldn't have increased their home loans as the value of their homes increased with the bubble, to burn this borrowed money on luxury; had these people been surfers, they would have had a financial buffer to pay the mortgage with during tougher economic periods, instead of - through foreclosure – being the bricks that fell out from the foundation and eventually caused the crash of the financial system.

And instability in the economy is indeed no joke. Right-wing undemocratic parties have grown dramatically in most European countries after the financial crisis of 2008, and even if we perhaps haven't experienced it ourselves we have read about how despotic leaders have managed to come to power in debilitated economies, as Hitler did in the 30s in Germany where hyperinflation and rampant unemployment raged. The lower probability of instability in the economy resulting from surfing the wave and its associated lifestyle is something we ought to highly value.

*

Finally, I would like to answer objections to Surf the Wave on a societal scale with the general comment that it would not be dangerous to give it a try. Surf the Wave would come from below, from the desire of individuals to improve their lives, and it would come slowly. Large and radical societal changes that have culminated in failure, even if the original idea was to improve the lives of people – for example those introduced by Lenin in Russia, Castro in Cuba and Pol Pot in Cambodia to mention a few – have on the contrary been characterized by coming from above, from the ideas of a small group of people about how others should live, and of being imposed rapidly. Despite good intentions, these experiments have resulted in brutality and human misery. Surf the Wave also represents large and radical changes, but because it takes time to build up a wave the consequences at a societal level occur slowly, giving time for errors to be corrected. And because the decision to build a wave is taken by the individuals themselves, the military machinery of the rulers does not have to be put in use to guarantee the project's progress. Although it's unclear today how society and the economy would function if all or a larger part of the population choose to surf the wave, the surfer lifestyle harbors good potential for both the wellbeing of individuals and as a con-tribution to solutions of serious contemporary problems, particularly those related to environ-mental and financial issues. And it would not be dangerous to explore this alternative.

This text was originally written for my teenage cousins who will soon leave compulsory education and embark into the adult world. The map they will have for this journey, however, will probably lack an important piece of information: That a financial wave to surf exists with which their working life doesn't need to be longer than 10 years. Had someone informed me about this when I was about to climb aboard on the same journey, my ride would not have been so bumpy and confused, although I haven't gone into the ditch like many other people.

I now want to share this enlightenment-writing with all young people out there to help them get the chance to start their adventure with a complete map. The present writing was created within a Swedish setting, but the idea of riding a financial wave is universal to people of all nationalities.

Kibo Hut
Stockholm, autumn 2019

kibo@kibohut.com